CW00516470

The
Winning
Attitude

Kenneth Copeland

KENNETH
COPELAND
PUBLICATIONS

Unless otherwise noted, all scripture is from the *King James Version* of the Bible.

The Winning Attitude

ISBN-10 0-88114-791-5   30-0031
ISBN-13 978-0-88114-791-9

14 13 12 11 10 09   20 19 18 17 16 15

Kenneth Copeland Publications
Fort Worth, TX 76192-0001

For more information about Kenneth Copeland Ministries, call 800-600-7395 or visit www.kcm.org.

The Winning Attitude

You've probably heard it said, "It's not whether you win or lose, it's how you play the game."

Do you believe that?

I don't!

Man was created to be a winner. The Bible tells us so! In Genesis, for example, we read that man was originally put on earth as dominating lord (Genesis 1:26-30). God gave him dominion over the earth and everything that crept, flew, crawled and breathed there. In fact, man didn't even know what it meant to lose until he separated himself from God through disobedience in the Garden of Eden. It wasn't until then that man ran headlong into defeat. He was forced to accept failure as his lot in life, lowering himself to a subordinate position—a position he was never meant to occupy.

It's a sad story. But if you're a born-again child of God, I have good news. Your story has a happy ending. Through faith in Christ Jesus, you've been transformed from the inside out. You've been made a winner once again!

You may be thinking, *I don't feel like a winner.*

I feel like a loser—and I have plenty of failures in my life to prove it. If that's the case, don't worry. You just need a new attitude. And you can get it from the Word of God.

In the book of Ephesians, the Apostle Paul told the Church to be renewed in the spirit of their minds. That's what you need to do. Renew your mind to the Word of God—base your thinking on the fact that Jesus has overcome the world. Begin seeing yourself as a winner in Him!

I'm reminded here of something Gen. George Patton said. He was a great commander of the United States Army with a God-given insight into war, and knew how vital a winning attitude could be. Once while addressing his troops, he put it this way: "Some of you men have come with your minds made up to die for your country. That's not the way to win a war! The way to win a war is to make your enemy die for his!" Patton had his mind made up to win—and he knew dying wasn't the way to do it. He had a winning attitude.

But, you know what? You have an even better reason to have a winning attitude than the general did. *God* has guaranteed your success. Let me show you what I mean. Imagine you're about to tackle a really tough job. Before you even get started, God speaks to you right out loud and says, "I just want you to know, I'm going to personally see to it that this project you're working on succeeds." Wouldn't that give you a tremendous feeling of confidence? Even if you ran into some rough spots, you wouldn't worry about failing because you would have God's word that you were going to succeed. That would make it easy to have a winning attitude, wouldn't it?

Well, let me tell you something. You *do* have God's promise that you'll succeed. He said in His Word that you're an "overcomer"! In Him, you can overcome any problem the world throws your way.

Read 1 John 5:1-5:

> Whosoever believeth that Jesus is the Christ is born of God: and every one that loveth him that begat loveth him also that is begotten of him. By this we know that we love the children of God, when we love God, and keep his commandments. For this is the love of God, that we keep his commandments: and his commandments are not grievous. For

whatsoever is born of God overcometh the world: and this is the victory that overcometh the world, even our faith. Who is he that overcometh the world, but he that believeth that Jesus is the Son of God?

God is being unusually explanatory here. He doesn't normally give such in-depth explanations of things that are written in the Word of God. The reason: He intends that we take what He says by faith, go to Him, and allow the Holy Spirit to reveal it to our hearts. That way the devil isn't tipped off to what it means.

God wrote the Bible as a code book. The book of Proverbs says that God has hidden godly wisdom for His people. That's the way He wants it. But in this portion of Scripture, God goes an unusual step further and asks, "Who is he that overcometh the world?" In other words, God is spelling it out, so we can't possibly miss it. He is saying, "This is the way I see it—whatsoever is born of Me overcomes the world; and who is he that overcomes the world, but he that believes that Jesus is the

Christ, the Son of the living God?"

This statement can also be read another way: "None but those who believe that Jesus is the Christ will ever overcome the world." No matter how smart, how strong or how rich you become, you can never truly be a winner—you can never really overcome the world—without Jesus as your Lord.

That means this world will never be overcome by a government, a political system or a monetary system. Money will *never* overcome the world! When the Bible talks about "the world," it is speaking of the dominion of darkness, the god of this world, the evil spirit—Satan—that operates in the world. Without Jesus Christ as their Lord, no man or system will ever in any way, form or fashion, be able to overcome the world. It simply can't be done.

But, on the other hand, if you *are* born of Him, you have an absolute, perfect, God-given, blood-bought right to overcome every aspect of the world—everything it could possibly send your way!

It doesn't matter how much you *feel* like a loser. It doesn't matter how many times you've failed in the past. If you believe Jesus is the

Christ, the Son of the living God, then you've committed yourself to overcoming the world. *And* you've been given the power to do it. You've become more than a conqueror (Romans 8:37). If you believe the Word of God, then you should respond to every challenge by saying, "Well, praise God, I'm an overcomer!" That should be your attitude. Does having this attitude guarantee you won't have any more trouble? No! It simply means you can go through that trouble and emerge triumphant.

Jesus said in John 16:33, "These things I have spoken unto you, that *in me* ye might have peace. In the world ye shall have tribulation: but be of good cheer; *I have overcome the world.*" In other words, Jesus is saying, "The world will come at you with everything it has to offer, but don't worry about it—I've already beaten it—I've already overcome the world."

Now when Jesus said He had overcome the world, He wasn't referring to just 99 percent of it. He said, "I have overcome *the world.*" One hundred percent of it! It makes no difference what problems the world brings to your doorstep. Just turn to Jesus and you're guaranteed to conquer those problems because

He has already overcome every one.

There's something else in that scripture I want you to notice. Jesus said, "...that in me ye might have peace." He was teaching here about being one with Him and the Father, and telling us that our battles here on this earth don't have to keep us in turmoil. He has guaranteed our victory, so if we'll just trust in Him, we can have peace, even in the midst of trouble.

When Jesus said these things, He was speaking to His disciples—men who had been with Him day and night for three years. Yet they couldn't grasp what it meant to be "in Him" as well as you and I can today. You see, the Holy Spirit had not yet come to dwell in them, and without the Holy Spirit, it's impossible to understand spiritual things. It takes the Holy Spirit to reveal even simple truths, like the reality of being born again.

Just think of it. These men had never even heard of being born again! Jesus told Nicodemus about it, but Nicodemus thought He was talking about a man going back into his mother's womb. Jesus told him, "I'm speaking of heavenly things, and you don't even understand earthly things." (See John 3:1-12.) These men had no concept of what Jesus was about to do at Calvary. They had no idea that through His death and resurrection, He was to become the firstborn from the dead and issue forth a new race of born-again winners filled with the mighty Spirit of God, Himself. Only after the Holy Spirit came on the Day of Pentecost could they see what Jesus had been saying. Then Peter stood up and boldly preached the Word of God by revelation of the Holy Spirit. Can you see what a change the Holy Spirit brought in his life?

Praise God, we *do* have the Holy Spirit to reveal to us the hidden truths in Jesus' words. So, let's look in John 17 at the last prayer Jesus prayed for His disciples before He went to the cross. This prayer is especially important for us. Why? Look at verse 20. Jesus says, "I'm not praying just for these in front of Me, but also for everyone who will believe on Me through their word." All of us received Jesus as Lord by the word of one or more of these disciples—either directly or indirectly. That means Jesus was praying that prayer for you and me. So we need to pay close attention to it.

Let's begin with verse 13. "And now come I to thee; and these things I speak in the world, that they might have my joy fulfilled in themselves."

Verse 15 says, "I pray not that thou shouldest take them out of the world, but that thou shouldest keep them from the evil." Jesus' prayer indicates that we are to live *above* the evil in the world. This ties in with what He said earlier—that we would have tribulation in the world, but to be of good cheer because He had overcome the world. Yes, He wants us to live above the evil, above the trials and tests and tribulations of the world, though we are constantly surrounded by them. But how is that possible?

You'll find the answer in verse 17: "Sanctify them through thy truth: thy word is truth." In today's English, Jesus is saying, "Separate them with Your Word." The Word of God will separate you from the world. It is your sword. Arm yourself with it. It will fight a winning fight.

If you're still not totally convinced you're a winner, look at verses 20-21. Jesus says, "Neither pray I for these alone, but for them also which shall believe on me through their word; that they all may be one; as thou, Father, art in me, and I in thee, that they also may be one in us: that the world may believe that thou hast sent me." Did you catch that? Jesus said, "We're all going to be one." The Apostle Paul said the same thing in 1 Corinthians 6:17. "But he that is joined unto the Lord is one spirit." Another translation says, "But he who is joined to the Lord is one spirit with Him" *(New King James Version)*.

Think about that. You are one with Almighty God. Is He a loser? Of course not! He's the greatest winner of all time. And that makes you a winner. Take His innermost feelings into your heart, and conform your own will and attitudes to His.

How do you do that? By listening to and acting on His Word. This is a much higher calling and a greater form of life than just submitting yourself to God.

Is that possible? Yes! The Word says we are predestined to be conformed to His very image—to be one spirit with Him. It says we have the mind of Christ and are bone of His bone. Thank God, we're connected to Jesus—spirit, soul and body—through the Holy Spirit and by His Word. We are completely and totally ONE with Him, so let's put ourselves in His position for a moment.

Is there any part of your life God can't handle? Certainly not!

Have you ever caught God asleep? No, the Bible says He never slumbers.

Have you ever gone to Jesus with a problem

He didn't know how to solve? No.

Have you ever heard Jesus say, "Well, I thought I had overcome the world, but evidently I haven't"? No!

Well, we're one with Him. If that's His attitude, then praise God, it should be our attitude. We are overcomers with Him!

If I said, "All things are possible with God," everyone would smile and quickly agree. But the same Bible, the same Jesus, the same Word of God says, "All things are possible to him who believes" *(Mark 9:23, New King James Version)*. If you believe the first statement, then you have to believe the second.

You and I need to change our perspective in all this. We are one with Him, so we need to set our attitudes to match His. If we are one with Him in spirit, soul and body, then we ought to be one with Him in attitude as well!

What *is* Jesus' attitude? A good example is the Lord's Prayer (Matthew 6:9-13). It is full of outright confessions of faith. Look at verses 9-10: "Our Father which art in heaven, Hallowed be thy name. Thy kingdom come. Thy will be done in earth, as it is in heaven." This is a statement of faith that shows Jesus' winning attitude. He was standing there in the face of people who wanted to stone Him when He prayed that! He didn't say, "Father, if it be Your will…." He didn't just say, "Thy will be done." He said, "Your will be done in earth *as it is in heaven!*" Is there sickness, poverty and suffering in heaven? No! Then there shouldn't be any of it here on earth. Can you see His attitude in this? God doesn't have sickness in heaven, so He doesn't want any here on earth!

Our attitude needs to be the same as His. Jesus is the eternal winner—He always wins! God can tell you what will happen 6,000 years from now. Why? Because the events taking place in the next 6,000 years or the next 6 million years will not happen just by chance. They are established. Where? In the mind of God. He has faith operating in His own ability. He is a faith being. He can tell you what will happen in the future because He intends for it to come out that way! He can give you His wisdom because it's going to be the way He decides.

How does He do it? With His faith. He doesn't expect to fail. He doesn't prepare to fail. Satan will get in and try to destroy things, but God doesn't worry—He knows it will come out all right. That's how we're to be. Roll all your cares over on

Him. Don't be moved by what you feel or by what you see. You're a faith person, so you know how things are going to come out. You're going to win, praise God!

The Church—the Body of Christ—has lived far below her privileges. We have lived as far below our spiritual privileges as Israel has lived below her political privileges. Israel should be the head and not the tail. She should not have to borrow from any nation on earth, and every nation on earth should be indebted to her. That's what God said. Well, that's how far below our spiritual privileges the Body of Christ has lived.

Through the years, God has exercised His faith for us. He has been willing to work for more than 2,000 years to get His plan functioning properly. The whole time the world lay in darkness, God was still believing—still exercising faith—not in just Himself, but in you and in me.

> That we henceforth be no more children, tossed to and fro, and carried about with every wind of doctrine, by the sleight of men, and cunning craftiness, whereby they lie in wait to deceive; but speaking the truth

in love, may grow up into him in all things, which is the head, even Christ: From whom the whole body fitly joined together and compacted by that which every joint supplieth... (Ephesians 4:14-16).

It's important to notice in this scripture the Lord didn't say *He* would hold the Body of Christ together. He said He would join it together, but that it would be held together, or compacted, by that which *every joint supplies*. He had to believe that you and I would supply what it took to hold the Body together. We've failed and failed and we've failed again, but God has kept on joining and believing. He has never uttered words of failure. Theology cries, "The Church is failing!" God says, "My house will be full, and the gates of hell will not prevail against it!" Religion is failing—God isn't! Can you see His attitude?

Look again at the verse, and you'll see how very important it is to the Body of Christ that you develop a winning attitude: "...compacted by that which every joint supplieth, according to the effectual working in the measure of every part" (verse 16). The Body of Christ depends on the direct amount, or measure, that each joint supplies. The amount you supply—the power you supply—affects the entire plan of God. Whether you supply some or much—affects the entire Body of Christ.

Verse 16 says, "according to the effectual working in the measure of every part, maketh increase of the body unto the edifying of itself in love." Here again, you can see your importance as an individual. God will not build up the Body. The members (you and I) must build up each other. Some are waiting for Jesus to return so the Body will rise without spot or wrinkle at the resurrection. But the Body of Christ is rising now, and the Bible says He will present to Himself a Body that is without spot or wrinkle. This will happen as His Body edifies itself in love, growing up into Him, and being washed by the water of the Word.

You can't afford to think like a loser. Change your attitude. The whole Body of Christ is counting on you. There will be times when you'll run into trouble, times when it looks like failure is inevitable. But follow your Father's example and keep believing that you're going to win. You know, during the Dark Ages, even though God had given His written Word, it had been shoved deep into monasteries, and the people couldn't reach it. Few if any, were being born again. It appeared as though God's plan was failing. But He didn't give up. He kept on believing.

There was enough faith in God's winning attitude to reach a little Catholic priest named Martin Luther. He began to scratch in the Word and found a sentence, "The just shall live by faith" (Romans 1:17). He found God through that one little sentence and generated enough power to begin a revival that is still going!

God had a winning attitude, and He refused to let go! Today the gospel is being preached in every nation on the face of the earth!

Remember, you're one with Him in the spirit, you have the mind of Christ and you're bone of His bone, so you might as well be attitude of His attitude! He sees you as an overcomer, so you need to see yourself that way too!

One time the Lord showed me a vision of a man holding a big banana. The man began to peel the banana, and as he did, I saw that there was no banana inside, but standing in the bottom was a little man. That little man was me! The Lord said, *Son, that's your attitude toward yourself.* It was true. I presented a big front to the world but actually felt very small on the inside. The Lord told me I needed to change my whole attitude.

He began to show me from His Word what it meant to be *in Christ* and to have Him in me. I began to see that a born-again believer is a limitless creature of God—an unlimited powerhouse of the very life of God, Himself! You need to realize this is your life. Allow God to supernaturally change your attitude. Allow Him to reveal Himself to you and give you this winning attitude—this world-overcoming attitude—in Jesus Christ!

Prayer for Salvation and Baptism in the Holy Spirit

Heavenly Father, I come to You in the Name of Jesus. Your Word says, "Whosoever shall call on the name of the Lord shall be saved" (Acts 2:21). I am calling on You. I pray and ask Jesus to come into my heart and be Lord over my life according to Romans 10:9-10: "If thou shalt confess with thy mouth the Lord Jesus, and shalt believe in thine heart that God hath raised him from the dead, thou shalt be saved. For with the heart man believeth unto righteousness; and with the mouth confession is made unto salvation." I do that now. I confess that Jesus is Lord, and I believe in my heart that God raised Him from the dead.

I am now reborn! I am a Christian—a child of Almighty God! I am saved! You also said in Your Word, "If ye then, being evil, know how to give good gifts unto your children: HOW MUCH MORE shall your heavenly Father give the Holy Spirit to them that ask him?" (Luke 11:13). I'm also asking You to fill me with the Holy Spirit. Holy Spirit, rise up within me as I praise God. I fully expect to speak with other tongues as You give me the utterance (Acts 2:4). In Jesus' Name. Amen!

Begin to praise God for filling you with the Holy Spirit. Speak those words and syllables you receive—not in your own language, but the language given to you by the Holy Spirit. You have to use your own voice. God will not force you to speak. Don't be concerned with how it sounds. It is a heavenly language!

Continue with the blessing God has given you and pray in the spirit every day.

You are a born-again, Spirit-filled believer. You'll never be the same!

Find a good church that boldly preaches God's Word and obeys it. Become part of a church family who will love and care for you as you love and care for them.

We need to be connected to each other. It increases our strength in God. It's God's plan for us.

Make it a habit to watch the *Believer's Voice of Victory* television broadcast and become a doer of the Word, who is blessed in his doing (James 1:22-25).

About the Author

Kenneth Copeland is co-founder and president of Kenneth Copeland Ministries in Fort Worth, Texas, and best-selling author of books that include *How to Discipline Your Flesh* and *Honor—Walking in Honesty, Truth and Integrity.*

Now in his 41st year as a minister of the gospel of Christ and teacher of God's Word, Kenneth is the recording artist of such award-winning albums as his Grammy-nominated *Only the Redeemed, In His Presence, He Is Jehovah, Just a Closer Walk* and his most recently released *Big Band Gospel* album. He also co-stars as the character Wichita Slim in the children's adventure videos *The Gunslinger, Covenant Rider* and the movie *The Treasure of Eagle Mountain,* and as Daniel Lyon in the *Commander Kellie and the Superkids*SM videos *Armor of Light* and *Judgment: The Trial of Commander Kellie.*

With the help of offices and staff in the United States, Canada, England, Australia, South Africa and Ukraine, Kenneth is fulfilling his vision to boldly preach the uncompromised Word of God from the top of this world, to the bottom, and all the way around. His ministry reaches millions of people worldwide through daily and Sunday TV broadcasts, magazines, teaching audios and videos, conventions and campaigns, and the World Wide Web.

Learn more about Kenneth Copeland Ministries
by visiting our Web site at **www.kcm.org**

Books Available From
Kenneth Copeland Ministries

by Kenneth Copeland

*   A Ceremony of Marriage
    A Matter of Choice
    Covenant of Blood
    Faith and Patience—The Power Twins
*   Freedom From Fear
    Giving and Receiving
    Honor—Walking in Honesty, Truth and Integrity
    How to Conquer Strife
    How to Discipline Your Flesh
    How to Receive Communion
    In Love There Is No Fear
    Know Your Enemy
    Living at the End of Time—A Time of
        Supernatural Increase
    Love Letters From Heaven
    Love Never Fails
*   Mercy—The Divine Rescue of the Human Race
*   Now Are We in Christ Jesus
    One Nation Under God (gift book with CD enclosed)
*   Our Covenant With God
    Partnership—Sharing the Vision, Sharing the Grace
*   Prayer—Your Foundation for Success
*   Prosperity: The Choice Is Yours
    Rumors of War
*   Sensitivity of Heart
*   Six Steps to Excellence in Ministry
*   Sorrow Not! Winning Over Grief and Sorrow
*   The Decision Is Yours

* The Force of Faith
* The Force of Righteousness
  The Image of God in You
  The Laws of Prosperity
  The Outpouring of the Spirit—The Result of Prayer
* The Power of the Tongue
  The Power to Be Forever Free
* The Winning Attitude
  Turn Your Hurts Into Harvests
  Walking in the Realm of the Miraculous
* Welcome to the Family
* You Are Healed!
  Your Right-Standing With God

by Gloria Copeland

* And Jesus Healed Them All
  Are You Listening?
  Are You Ready?
  Be a Vessel of Honor
  Blessed Beyond Measure
  Build Your Financial Foundation
  Fight On!
  God Has Your Miracle on His Mind
  God's Master Plan for Your Life
  God's Prescription for Divine Health
  God's Success Formula
  God's Will for You
  God's Will for Your Healing
  God's Will Is Prosperity
* God's Will Is the Holy Spirit
  Go With the Flow
* Harvest of Health
* Hearing From Heaven

* Available in Spanish

Hidden Treasures
Living in Heaven's Blessings Now
Looking for a Receiver
* Love—The Secret to Your Success
No Deposit—No Return
Pleasing the Father
Pressing In—It's Worth It All
Shine On!
The Grace That Makes Us Holy
The Power to Live a New Life
The Protection of Angels
There Is No High Like the Most High
The Secret Place of God's Protection (gift book with
        CD enclosed)
The Unbeatable Spirit of Faith
This Same Jesus
To Know Him
True Prosperity
Walk With God
Well Worth the Wait
Words That Heal (gift book with CD enclosed)
Your Promise of Protection—The Power
    of the 91st Psalm

Books Co-Authored by Kenneth and Gloria Copeland

Family Promises
Healing Promises
Prosperity Promises
Protection Promises

* From Faith to Faith—A Daily Guide to Victory
From Faith to Faith—A Perpetual Calendar

He Did It All for You
One Word From God Can Change Your Life

One Word From God Series:
- One Word From God Can Change Your Destiny
- One Word From God Can Change Your Family
- One Word From God Can Change Your Finances
- One Word From God Can Change Your Formula
  for Success
- One Word From God Can Change Your Health
- One Word From God Can Change Your Nation
- One Word From God Can Change Your Prayer Life
- One Word From God Can Change
  Your Relationships

Load Up—A Youth Devotional
Over the Edge—A Youth Devotional
Pursuit of His Presence—A Daily Devotional
Pursuit of His Presence—A Perpetual Calendar
Raising Children Without Fear

Other Books Published by KCP

John G. Lake—His Life, His Sermons, His
    Boldness of Faith
The Holiest of All by Andrew Murray
The New Testament in Modern Speech
    by Richard Francis Weymouth
The Rabbi From Burbank by Isidor Zwirn and Bob Owen
Unchained! by Mac Gober

* Available in Spanish

Products Designed for Today's Children and Youth

And Jesus Healed Them All (confession book and CD gift package)
Baby Praise Board Book
Baby Praise Christmas Board Book
Noah's Ark Coloring Book
The Best of *Shout!* Adventure Comics
The *Shout!* Giant Flip Coloring Book
The *Shout!* Joke Book
The *Shout!* Super-Activity Book
Wichita Slim's Campfire Stories

Commander Kellie and the Superkids_{SM} **Books:**

The SWORD Adventure Book
*Commander Kellie and the Superkids*_{SM}
    Solve-It-Yourself Mysteries
*Commander Kellie and the Superkids*_{SM} Adventure Series:
    Middle Grade Novels by Christopher P.N. Maselli:

    #1 The Mysterious Presence
    #2 The Quest for the Second Half
    #3 Escape From Jungle Island
    #4 In Pursuit of the Enemy
    #5 Caged Rivalry
    #6 Mystery of the Missing Junk
    #7 Out of Breath
    #8 The Year Mashela Stole Christmas
    #9 False Identity
    #10 The Runaway Mission
    #11 The Knight-Time Rescue of Commander Kellie

World Offices
Kenneth Copeland Ministries

For more information about KCM and our products, please
write to the office nearest you:

Kenneth Copeland Ministries
Fort Worth, TX 76192-0001

Kenneth Copeland
Locked Bag 2600
Mansfield Delivery Centre
QUEENSLAND 4122
AUSTRALIA

Kenneth Copeland
Post Office Box 15
BATH
BA1 3XN
U.K.

Kenneth Copeland
Private Bag X 909
FONTAINEBLEAU
2032
REPUBLIC OF
SOUTH AFRICA

Kenneth Copeland
PO Box 3111 STN LCD 1
Langley BC V3A 4R3
CANADA

Kenneth Copeland Ministries
Post Office Box 84
L'VIV 79000
UKRAINE

We're Here for You!

Believer's Voice of Victory Television Broadcast

Join Kenneth and Gloria Copeland and the *Believer's Voice of Victory* broadcasts Monday through Friday and on Sunday each week, and learn how faith in God's Word can take your life from ordinary to extraordinary. This teaching from God's Word is designed to get you where you want to be—*on top!*

You can catch the *Believer's Voice of Victory* broadcast on your local, cable or satellite channels.* Also available 24 hours on webcast at BVOV.TV.

*Check your local listings for times and stations in your area.

Believer's Voice of Victory Magazine

Enjoy inspired teaching and encouragement from Kenneth and Gloria Copeland and guest ministers each month in the *Believer's Voice of Victory* magazine. Also included are real-life testimonies of God's miraculous power and divine intervention in the lives of people just like you!

It's more than just a magazine—it's a ministry.

To receive a FREE subscription to
Believer's Voice of Victory, write to:

Kenneth Copeland Ministries
Fort Worth, TX 76192-0001
Or call:
800-600-7395
(7 a.m.-5 p.m. CT)
Or visit our Web site at:
www.kcm.org

If you are writing from outside the U.S., please contact the
KCM office nearest you. Addresses for all Kenneth Copeland
Ministries offices are listed on the previous pages.